For the Teacher

This reproducible study guide to use in conjunction with the novel *The Miraculous Journey of Edward Tulane* consists of lessons for guided reading. Written in chapter-by-chapter format, the guide contains a synopsis, pre-reading activities, vocabulary and comprehension exercises, as well as extension activities to be used as follow-up to the novel.

In a homogeneous classroom, whole class instruction with one title is appropriate. In a heterogeneous classroom, reading groups should be formed: each group works on a different novel at its own reading level. Depending upon the length of time devoted to reading in the classroom, each novel, with its guide and accompanying lessons, may be completed in three to six weeks.

Begin using NOVEL-TIES for reading development by distributing the novel and a folder to each child. Distribute duplicated pages of the study guide for students to place in their folders. After examining the cover and glancing through the book, students can participate in several pre-reading activities. Vocabulary questions should be considered prior to reading a chapter; all other work should be done after the chapter has been read. Comprehension questions can be answered orally or in writing. The classroom teacher should determine the amount of work to be assigned, always keeping in mind that readers must be nurtured and that the ultimate goal is encouraging students' love of reading.

The benefits of using NOVEL-TIES are numerous. Students read good literature in the original, rather than in abridged or edited form. The good reading habits, formed by practice in focusing on interpretive comprehension and literary techniques, will be transferred to the books students read independently. Passive readers become active, avid readers.

Novel-Ties® are printed on recycled paper.

SYNOPSIS

Edward Tulane, an expensive china rabbit, lives with a girl named Abilene who loves him dearly. She dresses him in elegant clothes and regards him as her special friend. But Edward does not feel love in return: he is too impressed with himself to care much about anyone else. Only one person, Abilene's grandmother Pellegrina, sees through Edward: she knows he is puffed up with self-importance. So she tells him a somber fairy tale designed to frighten Edward and teach him a lesson.

When the family goes abroad on the Queen Mary, Edward attracts the attention of the other children on the ship. In a rough game of catch, Edward tumbles overboard and sinks to the bottom of the ocean. There he lies in misery until a fisherman's net lifts him out of the sea. Edward Tulane's adventures have begun.

Lawrence, the fisherman, brings him home to his wife Nellie, who is grieving for a child who has died. Nellie and Lawrence make Edward comfortable in their home. But when the couple's begrudging daughter discards the rabbit in the trash, Edward is once again homeless and alone. Time passes, and a hobo's dog digs Edward out of the garbage dump. Edward goes on the road with Bull, the hobo, and his dog Lucy. The china rabbit, no longer neatly dressed and elegant, rides the rails and camps out with the other hoboes, adapting well enough to this life before an irate worker tosses him off a moving train. An old woman discovers him in the dirt and gives him a job as a scarecrow. Utterly humiliated and friendless, Edward is now in the depths of despair. He has begun to understand the emptiness of a life without connection to others.

Edward gets another chance when a poor country boy named Bryce rescues him from the field and brings him home to Sarah Ruth, his dying sister. Before the little girl succumbs to her terrible illness, Edward learns what it is to return love. Having once again lost someone special to him, Edward sets out on the road with Bryce, who is running away from his father's cruelty. On the streets of Memphis, the boy and the rabbit, now a puppet, entertain the passersby for spare change. When Bryce is unable to pay the full price of a diner meal, the cook takes his revenge on Edward, cracking his head open against a counter.

It seems that everything is over for Edward, but Bryce nobly gives up possession of the china rabbit to an expert doll mender named Lucius Clarke. Repaired and made handsome again, though bearing the scars of his battering, Edward now finds himself on a shelf of dolls in Lucius Clarke's toy store. Edward's heart closes against the hard world as years pass and no one comes to claim him. But a very old doll assures him that someone will come in time, and Edward dares to hope again. One miraculous day, a grownup Abilene Tulane and her young daughter Maggie come into the shop and take Edward home with them to a world of caring and affection.

PRE-READING QUESTIONS AND ACTIVITIES

1. Preview the book by reading the title and the author's name and by looking at the illustration on the cover. When and where do you think this story takes place?

2. The main character in this story is not a person, but a china rabbit with thoughts and feelings. Have you read any other books or stories in which the most important character is an animal or other nonhuman being? When you finish reading *The Miraculous Journey of Edward Tulane*, compare the characters in these other stories with the character of Edward.

3. In this novel, the main character goes on a journey that helps him discover some important truths. What might someone learn on a journey marked by hardship, despair, and loss? How do you suppose that good could come out of suffering?

4. This story takes place during a time when children played with simpler toys—no computers, video games, or remote-control cars. What do you think such a world would be like? Do you have any simple toys or games that are special to you? Why?

5. **Art/Social Studies Connection:** Do some research to find out about the art of making fine china dolls and toys. How were these dolls manufactured in the past? What makes these objects collectibles? Find some photographs of these objects and share them with the class.

6. **Pair/Share:** With a partner, discuss some of the important relationships in your own life. What have you learned from each of these relationships?

7. Flip through *The Miraculous Journey of Edward Tulane* and study the illustrations. What does the artwork reveal to you about the book? Choose one illustration and write a description of what you see. Exchange descriptions with another person who is getting ready to read the same book.

8. **Social Studies Connection:** Some of the characters in this novel live in great poverty. There are hints in the story that part of the action is set during "The Great Depression," a time of economic hardship for the United States and many other nations. With a partner, discuss how people can manage to survive with little income. How might people adapt to a life of poverty?

9. Read the statements in the Anticipation Guide on page three of this study guide. In the "You" column, place a [✓] next to each statement with which you agree. When you finish the story, place a check next to each statement with which you think the author would agree.

10. As you read *The Miraculous Journey of Edward Tulane*, fill in the story map on page four of this study guide.

Pre-Reading Questions and Activities (cont.)

ANTICIPATION GUIDE

Statement	You	Author
1. If you cannot feel love, you are not truly alive.		
2. Loving others too much makes people needy.		
3. Difficult experiences can make us wiser.		
4. The clothing we wear shows who we really are.		
5. It is possible to get used to many different ways of life.		
6. Those who don't like us don't really understand us.		
7. Memories can last for an entire lifetime.		
8. Gentleness is often a sign of weakness.		
9. Without hope, a person cannot survive.		
10. All wounds heal with enough time.		

Pre-Reading Questions and Activities (cont.)

STORY MAP

Title _____

Author _____

Main Characters	Descriptions

Plot—Main Events

First, _____

_____

Then, _____

_____

_____

Next, _____

_____

Finally, _____

_____

Theme—Message

This story taught me that _____

_____

_____

CHAPTERS 1 – 4

Vocabulary: Draw a line from each word on the left to its definition on the right. Then use the numbered words to fill in the blanks in the sentences below.

1.	jaunty	a.	suggestions
2.	specimen	b.	industry; attention
3.	unsavory	c.	ugly; absurd
4.	duration	d.	lively or self-confident
5.	china	e.	example or type
6.	implications	f.	disagreeable or distasteful
7.	diligence	g.	length of time something continues
8.	grotesque	h.	ceramic material, usually used to make plates

. . . .

1. Because of its messy tables and dirty floors, we left the _____ restaurant in order to find some place more appealing.

2. If you want to run in the statewide competition, you will have to attend track practice for the _____ of the year.

3. The children were frightened by the _____ Halloween mask.

4. The fire was put out quickly with little damage to the building because the firefighters performed their work with great _____.

5. At first, many people did not understand the _____ of the Wright brothers flying machine, but we now know that it meant the beginning of the age of flight.

6. When you are shipping _____ plates through the mail, it is important to pack them carefully so they do not break.

7. The little poodle trotted down the street with a(n) _____ air.

8. We found a perfect _____ of a starfish on our beach walk.

> Read to find out why Edward, a china rabbit, lives with the Tulane family.

Chapters 1 – 4 (cont.)

Questions:

1. What evidence showed that Abilene thought Edward was "real"?

2. Why didn't Edward like Abilene's parents?

3. Why was Edward always awake?

4. How did Edward react to Rosie's attack?

5. Why was Edward upset by the maid's treatment of him?

6. Why was Abilene unhappy with the ending of Pellegrina's story?

7. What did Pellegrina understand about Edward's true nature? Did Abilene really understand Edward, too?

Questions for Discussion:

1. Why do you suppose the story begins "Once, in a house on Egypt Street"? What kinds of stories have a similar beginning?

2. Why do you think Edward had such a high opinion of himself?

3. Do you think that Edward was a likeable rabbit? Did he deserve Abilene's affection?

4. Why do you suppose Pellegrina had given Edward to Abilene as a birthday gift? Why might Abilene have needed the china rabbit?

5. What do you think was the message or moral of Pellegrina's story?

6. Why do you think Edward was disturbed by the story of the princess?

Literary Devices:

I. *Foreshadowing*—Foreshadowing refers to the clues or hints an author provides to suggest what will happen later in the novel. What might be foreshadowed at the end of Chapter Two?

_____

_____

Chapters 1 – 4 (cont.)

II. *Analogy*—An analogy in literature is a comparison between two or more similar objects so as to suggest that if they are alike in some ways, they will probably be alike in other ways as well. For example, when the family discusses taking a trip, Edward becomes aware that Pellegrina is studying him:

> She was looking at him in the way a hawk hanging lazily in the air might study a mouse on the ground.

What is being compared?

_____

_____

What do these two experiences have in common?

_____

_____

III. *Simile*—A simile is a figure of speech in which two unlike objects are compared using the words "like" or "as." For example:

> She shone as bright as the stars on a moonlit night.

What is being compared?

_____

_____

What does this tell you about the princess?

_____

_____

Writing Activities:

1. Imagine that you are Abilene and rewrite the ending of the Princess's story as you would like it to be.

2. Write about a toy or other object that you love. Describe this treasure and explain why it is special to you.

CHAPTERS 5 – 9

Vocabulary: Use the context to determine the meaning of the underlined word in each of the following sentences. Then compare your definitions to a dictionary definition.

1. When the horse saw the snake near its legs, the large creature became <u>frantic</u> with fear.

   Your definition _____

   Dictionary definition _____

2. The huge Statue of Liberty, which seems to rise out of New York's harbor, is a <u>singular</u> sight.

   Your definition _____

   Dictionary definition _____

3. I felt <u>mortified</u> when I forgot my lines in the class play.

   Your definition _____

   Dictionary definition _____

4. While the hardworking ant piled up food for the winter, the lazy grasshopper <u>blithely</u> went on playing.

   Your definition _____

   Dictionary definition _____

5. As the airplane began its <u>descent</u>, we could once again see trees and tiny houses dotting the land.

   Your definition _____

   Dictionary definition _____

6. The storm at sea was so bad that it lifted up the boat and then <u>pummeled</u> it back down again.

   Your definition _____

   Dictionary definition _____

7. A <u>discerning</u> shopper will look carefully at an item before making a purchase.

   Your definition _____

   Dictionary definition _____

> Read to find out how Edward became Susanna.

Chapters 5 – 9 (cont.)

Questions:

1. Why was Edward glad that Pellegrina was not going on the trip?
2. How did Edward end up at the bottom of the ocean?
3. Why did Edward feel his first "genuine and true emotion"?
4. How was Edward rescued?
5. What confused Edward about Nellie's response to him?
6. What terrible sadness had Nellie experienced?
7. How did Edward feel about life with Nellie and Lawrence? Why was he able to adjust to the new life so easily?
8. Whom did Edward blame for his troubles? Why?
9. How did Lawrence show fondness for "Susanna"?

Questions for Discussion:

1. In what ways do you think Edward was changing?
2. Why do you suppose Nellie enjoyed having a china rabbit to talk to, dress up, and fuss over?
3. Do you think what happened to Edward was an accident, or was there a reason for these events?

Literary Devices:

I. *Foreshadowing*—What do you think is being foreshadowed at the end of Chapter Nine?

_____

_____

II. *Point of View*—Point of view in literature refers to the voice telling the story. The story may be told by a character (first-person narrative) or by the author (third-person narrative). From whose point of view is *The Miraculous Journey of Edward Tulane* told? Why do you suppose the author chose this point of view?

_____

_____

_____

Chapters 5 – 9 (cont.)

Literary Element: Setting

The setting of a work of literature refers to the time and place in which the story unfolds. The setting of a story may change several times. How does each setting in the book so far shape Edward's experiences and feelings?

_____

_____

_____

_____

_____

Social Studies Connection:

Do some research to find out about the ship called the *Queen Mary*. When was the ship built? What were its routes? What other interesting facts can you discover about this ocean liner? Prepare a short oral report and share your findings with a group of classmates.

Science Connection:

Lawrence enjoys pointing out special sights in the night sky. Do some research to learn about the North Star and the constellations of Andromeda and Pegasus. Find out how to locate them in the sky and learn how far each object or group of objects is from the earth.

Music Connection:

Go online to *www.mamalisa.com* to read the words and hear the lullabye *Hush Little Baby* that Nellie sang to Edward. Do some additional research to find out about the origin of this lullabye.

Writing Activities:

1. Write about a time when you were far from home. How did you feel about this experience? Were you homesick, or did you enjoy the adventure?

2. Describe an experience that changed you. What happened? How did this experience help you grow or change?

CHAPTERS 10 – 15

Vocabulary: Synonyms are words with similar meanings. Draw a line from each word in column A to its synonym in column B. Then use the words in column A to fill in the blanks in the sentences below.

A	B
1. abiding	a. lasting
2. rancid	b. excited
3. savor	c. spoiled
4. exhilarated	d. clothing
5. resonated	e. echoed
6. garb	f. enjoy

. . . .

1. When the first lovely flakes of snow fell, the children were _____.

2. The shouts of the lost explorers _____ off the cave walls.

3. My uncle has a deep and _____ love of nature.

4. We ate ice cream slowly so we could _____ its delicious taste.

5. The actor appeared in the _____ of a beggar with a threadbare coat and torn trousers.

6. It is important to refrigerate dairy products so that they do not become _____.

> Read to find out how Edward's life changes over and over again.

Questions:

1. Why did Edward form an immediate hatred for Lolly, Nellie's daughter?

2. Why did Lolly take Edward to the dump?

3. What made Edward realize that he had changed?

4. How was Edward rescued from the garbage dump?

Chapters 10 – 15 (cont.)

5. How did Edward, now named Malone, take to the road with a hobo?

6. What was unusual about Bull's journey?

7. Why did Bull change Edward's clothes?

8. How did listening to other people's stories open Edward's heart?

9. After being together for seven years, how was Edward separated from Bull?

10. What made Edward feel that he was "done with caring"?

Questions for Discussion:

1. Why do you think Nellie and Lawrence let their daughter bully them?

2. Why do you think Bull wanted Edward to stay with him? Have you ever known an adult who treasured a doll?

3. Why do you suppose the hoboes whispered the names of their children in Edward's ear?

4. Why do you think Edward wished he could cry? What did this reveal about him?

Literary Devices:

I. *Onomatopoeia*—Onomatopoeia is a literary device in which a word imitates a sound found in nature. For instance, the word *crash* imitates the sound of one object hitting another. Which words in these sentences are examples of onomatopoeia?

   • They clinked and clanked and shone in the morning sun.

   • They came flying at him, cawing and screeching, wheeling over his head, diving at his ears.

   Work with a partner to make a list of other words that are examples of onomatopoeia.

II. *Cliffhanger*—A cliffhanger is a device borrowed from serialized silent films in which an episode ends at a moment of suspense. In a book it usually appears at the end of a chapter to encourage the reader to go on in the book. What is the cliffhanger at the end of Chapter Fifteen?

_____

_____

Chapters 10 – 15 (cont.)

Literary Element: Mood

Mood in literature refers to the atmosphere or state of mind produced by a passage. Mood also helps the reader guess what is to follow. Read this passage from *The Miraculous Journey of Edward Tulane*:

> On his one hundred and eightieth day at the dump, salvation arrived for Edward in a most unusual form. The garbage around him shifted, and the rabbit heard the sniffing and panting of a dog. Then came the frenzied sound of digging. The garbage shifted again, and suddenly, miraculously, the beautiful, buttery light of late afternoon shone on Edward's face.

What mood does the passage create? What were your feelings as you read this description of a meaningful moment for Edward? Underline the words that helped suggest this mood.

_____

_____

Social Studies Connection:

Do some research to learn more about the people we call "hoboes." What makes a person a hobo? Which periods of American history produced the largest number of homeless people on the move? Why? Prepare a short oral report for a group of your classmates.

Writing Activity:

Imagine that you are Edward Tulane and you wish to express your new emotions to Abilene. Write a note to her telling her where you have been, whom you have been with, and what you think will happen next.

CHAPTERS 16 – 19

Vocabulary: Antonyms are words with opposite meanings. Draw a line from each word on the left to its antonym on the right. Then use the numbered words to fill in the blanks in the sentences below.

1. loathed   a. respectful
2. provoked   b. accepted
3. murmured   c. definite
4. intrusive   d. loved
5. ignored   e. calmed
6. tentative   f. shouted
7. refused   g. failed
8. prevailed   h. responded

. . . .

1. I _____ the ringing telephone because I did not want to stop eating my dinner.

2. It rained all morning, but in the afternoon, the sunshine finally _____.

3. The closing of the town's main playground _____ a storm of protest from children and their parents.

4. My sister _____ the movie, but I really enjoyed it.

5. The reporter's _____ questions annoyed the scientist, who wanted to keep his methods a secret.

6. The young child's first footsteps were _____, but soon she became more sure of her strength.

7. "Go to sleep," the mother _____ gently to her tired daughter.

8. I _____ to join the team because I did not want to be a beginner among a group of experienced players.

> Read to find out what happened to Bryce and Edward in Memphis.

Chapters 16 – 19 (cont.)

Questions:

1. Why did Bryce rescue Edward from his miserable job as a scarecrow?

2. Why did Edward respond happily to Sarah Ruth's attentions?

3. What new feeling did Edward experience while he was with Sarah Ruth? Why did he feel this way?

4. What evidence shows that Edward was living among poor people?

5. Why did Bryce attach strings to Edward?

6. In what ways was Bryce a father figure to Sarah Ruth?

7. Why did Bryce set off for Memphis? What had kept him at home for so long?

Questions for Discussion:

1. Do you think Edward was happier before he had feelings? Is it always good to have feelings for others? Or does it sometimes hurt?

2. Why do you suppose the father could not show love for his children?

3. Why do you imagine Edward did not object to being turned into a puppet or object to having his ear nibbled on by Sarah Ruth? What did this acceptance show about Edward?

4. Do you think that the father had really loved Sarah Ruth? In your opinion is it possible to mistreat and neglect someone you love?

5. Why do you think Bryce took Edward with him as he left for Memphis?

Literary Devices:

I. *Symbolism*—A symbol in literature is an object, person, or event that represents an idea of set of ideas. What do you think the stars symbolized for Edward?

_____

_____

Chapters 16 – 19 (cont.)

II. *Vernacular*—Vernacular refers to the common, everyday speech of people who live in a particular area. For example:

"Yours," said Bryce. "I got him special for you."

Dialogue like this makes characters seem real to us. What other examples of vernacular can you find in the novel?

_____

_____

_____

Writing Activity:

Imagine that Bryce loses Edward on the road and that you find the toy rabbit. Write about an imagined short journey that you make with Edward.

CHAPTER 20 – 23

Vocabulary: Use the words from the Word Box and the clues below to complete the crossword puzzle.

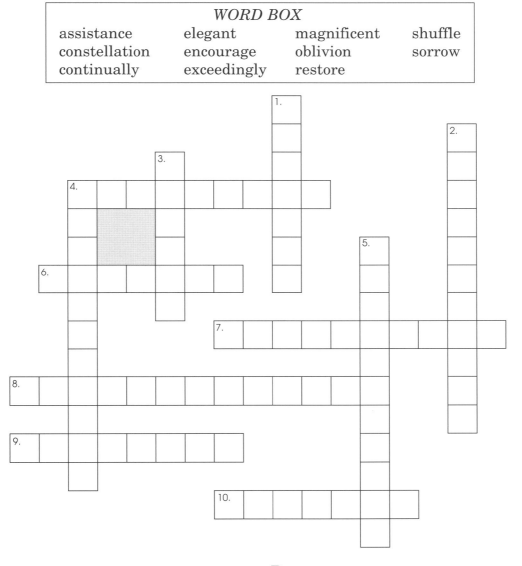

WORD BOX			
assistance	elegant	magnificent	shuffle
constellation	encourage	oblivion	sorrow
continually	exceedingly	restore	

Across
4. give hope or confidence
6. bring back to its original condition
7. help; aid
8. group of stars
9. state of forgetting or being forgotten
10. perform a dance; kind of dance

Down
1. tasteful or rich, especially in dress or furnishings
2. presenting a breathtaking appearance
3. sadness
4. unusually; extremely
5. without stopping

Chapters 20 – 23 (cont.)

> Read to find out how Edward found himself in the company of dolls.

Questions:

1. What made Edward feel hollow again?
2. Why did Bryce make Edward dance?
3. Why did Edward identify the old woman with the cane as Pellegrina?
4. Why did Neal swing Edward against the counter? What happened to Edward?
5. What did it mean that Edward's world "went black"?
6. How would you explain the events that took place in Chapter Twenty-two? What was really happening?
7. How did Bryce make a sacrifice for Edward?
8. Why did Lucius Clarke mend Edward?

Questions for Discussion:

1. Why do you suppose Bryce cried while performing on the street corner?
2. Do you agree with Edward that loving deeply may cause a person grief? Do you think a person should avoid love for that reason?
3. Why do you think Neal took out his anger and frustration on Edward?
4. Why do you think that love sometimes requires sacrifice? Have you ever known this to be true in your life or in the lives of people you know?
5. Do you think Edward will benefit from Lucius Clarke's repairs? Will the restoration of his body make him whole again?

Literary Element: Metaphor

A metaphor is a suggested or implied comparison between two unlike objects. For example:

> The sun became an orange dusty ball low in the sky.

What is being compared?

_____

How does the writer's use of figurative language help you to picture the end of the afternoon?

_____

Chapters 20 – 23 (cont.)

Art Connection:

Create an artwork that shows one of the events in this part of the novel. You might make a drawing, painting, collage, or sculpture. Place your artwork in the classroom so that others can enjoy it.

Social Studies Connection:

Do some research to find out about children who run away from home. What kinds of problems do young runaways face? What kinds of social services exist to help such children? Prepare a booklet on your findings. Share the booklet with your classmates.

Writing Activities:

1. Write about a time you made a plan that didn't work out as you had expected. Describe what happened.

2. Write about a time when you were treated unfairly. Tell how you dealt with this experience.

CHAPTERS 24 – CODA

Vocabulary: Read each group of words. Cross out the one that does not belong with the others. On the line below the word group, tell how the remaining words are alike.

1. mended   repaired   patched   shattered

   These words are alike because _____

2. vain   proud   self-important   glum

   These words are alike because _____

3. precious   plain   obvious   clear

   These words are alike because _____

4. impassioned   heated   intense   mild

   These words are alike because _____

5. unused   empty   vacant   occupied

   These words are alike because _____

6. disgusting   terrible   pleasant   horrid

   These words are alike because _____

7. jokingly   seriously   solemnly   gravely

   These words are alike because _____

8. robust   fragile   delicate   brittle

   These words are alike because _____

Read to learn how Edward found a home once again.

Questions:

1. Why didn't Lucius want Bryce to keep returning to his shop?
2. Why didn't Edward want anyone to buy him?
3. What did the hundred-year-old doll try to explain to Edward? Who else had tried to explain this to him?
4. What made Edward dare to hope for love again?
5. What made Abilene, now grown up, recognize Edward after many years?
6. Why did Abilene wear a pocket watch on a chain around her neck?
7. How did the story end "happily after after"?

Chapters 24 – Coda (cont.)

Questions for Discussion:

1. Do you think Abilene had changed greatly from the days of her childhood?

2. Which of Edward's experiences do you think helped him to see what was precious in life?

3. Why do you think the author used a china rabbit to tell a story about the value of love?

4. Some people say that hope is the most important emotion. Do you agree or disagree?

Literary Device:

I. *Symbolism*—What did Edward's pocket watch represent at the end of the story?

_____

_____

II. *Imagery*—Imagery in literature is created by the careful choice of descriptive words and comparisons. Writers use imagery to help readers picture a scene in their imaginations. Notice how the author uses imagery in this passage:

> Leaves blew in through the open door of Lucius Clarke's shop, and rain, and the green outrageous hopeful light of spring.

Which words in the passage help you to form a clear picture, or image, of the scene?

_____

_____

III. *Irony*—Irony is the difference between the way things seem to be and the way they actually are. What is ironic about Edward's distaste for dolls?

> Edward had never cared for dolls. He found them annoying and self-centered, twittery and vain.

_____

_____

Writing Activities:

1. Imagine that you are Abilene. Write a diary entry telling how you felt as you recognized Edward and bought him for your daughter.

2. Write about a real or imagined time when you met someone you thought you might never see again. Describe this experience and your feelings about it.

CLOZE ACTIVITY

The following passage is taken from Chapter Seven of the novel. Read it through completely, and then fill in each blank with a word that makes sense. Afterwards, you may compare your language with that of the author.

He told himself that certainly Abilene would come and find him. This, Edward

thought, is much like _____ [1] for Abilene to come home from _____. [2]

I will pretend that I am _____ [3] the dining room of the house _____ [4]

Egypt Street, waiting for the little _____ [5] to move to the three and

_____ [6] big hand to land on the _____. [7] If only I had my watch,

_____ [8] I would know for sure. But _____ [9] doesn't matter; she will

be here _____, [10] very soon.

Hours passed. And then _____. [11] And weeks. And months.

Abilene did _____ [12] come.

Edward, for lack of anything _____ [13] to do, began to think. He

_____ [14] about the stars. He remembered what _____ [15] looked like

from his bedroom window.

_____ [16] made them shine so brightly, he _____, [17] and

were they still shining somewhere _____ [18] though he could not see them?

Never in my life, he thought, have I been farther away from the stars than I am now.

POST-READING ACTIVITIES

1. Return to the Anticipation Guide that you began in the Pre-Reading Activities on page three of this study guide. Place a check next to each statement with which you think the author would agree. Then compare and discuss your responses with others who have read this book.

2. Return to the story map that you began in the Pre-Reading Activities on page four of this study guide. Fill in additional information and compare your responses with those of your classmates.

3. In a story, a conflict is a struggle between two opposing forces. In *The Miraculous Journey of Edward Tulane*, Edward and some of the other characters have conflicts they try to resolve. Many stories present more than one conflict. Use a chart, such as the one below, to list the conflicts explored in *The Miraculous Journey of Edward Tulane*.

Type of Conflict	Example
person *vs.* person/society	
person *vs.* nature	
person *vs.* self (inner struggle)	

4. Why do you think the novel was titled *The Miraculous Journey of Edward Tulane*? If you had to choose a different title for the book, what would it be?

5. Now that you have read the story, think again about what someone might learn from a difficult and challenging journey. What important discoveries did Edward make? Do you think he would have learned these lessons if he had remained in his comfortable life with Abilene?

6. **Pair/Share:** With a partner, discuss the significance of the Coda to the novel. Why do you think the author wrote this section? What does the story gain by having a Coda?

7. **Fluency/Readers Theater:** Read a chapter of the book that has a lot of dialogue. Each character's dialogue should be read by one student. The characters should read only those words inside the quotation marks. Ignore phrases such as "he said" or "she said." One student can read the narration. Use simple props, such as hats, to identify the characters.

8. **Literary Element/Theme:** Theme in literature refers to the author's message or the central story ideas. In *The Miraculous Journey of Edward Tulane*, the author explores several themes involving relationships and personal growth. Work with a partner to make a list of important themes. Compare your list to those of your classmates.

Post-Reading Activities (cont.)

9. Now that you have finished reading the novel, read the poem by Stanley Kunitz that appears at the beginning of the book. With a partner, discuss how this poem relates to Edward's experiences.

10. **Literature Circle:** Have a literature circle discussion in which you tell your personal reactions to *The Miraculous Journey of Edward Tulane*. Here are some questions and sentence starters to help your literature circle begin a discussion.
   - Which character in the novel are you most like? Why?
   - Which character did you like the most? The least?
   - Even though the story uses fantasy, do you find the characters in the novel believable? Why or why not?
   - Who else would like to read this novel? Why?
   - What questions would you like to ask the author about this novel?
   - It was not fair when . . .
   - I would have liked to see . . .
   - I wonder . . .
   - Edward learned that . . .

SUGGESTIONS FOR FURTHER READING

Bailey, Carolyn Sherwin. *Miss Hickory*. Penguin.

* Banks, Lynn Reid. *The Indian in the Cupboard*. HarperCollins.

Brooks, Walter R. *Freddy and the Perilous Adventure*. Random House.

Coatsworth, Elizabeth. *The Cat Who Went to Heaven*. Simon & Schuster.

* Dahl, Roald. *Charlie and the Chocolate Factory*. Penguin.

Field, Rachel. *Hitty, Her First Hundred Years*. Simon & Schuster.

Godden, Rumer. *The Doll's House*. Penguin.

Howe, Deborah and James Howe. *Bunnicula: A Rabbit Tale of Mystery*. HarperCollins.

Jarrell, Randall. *The Animal Family*. Random House.

* Juster, Norton. *The Phantom Tollbooth*. Random House.

Kennedy, Richard. *Amy's Eyes*. HarperCollins.

Mukerji, Dhan Gopal. *Gay-Neck: The Story of a Pigeon*. Penguin

* Norton, Mary. *The Borrowers*. Harcourt.

* Selden, George. *The Cricket in Times Square*. Random House.

* Steig, William. *Abel's Island*. Farrar, Straus, and Giroux.

* White, E.B. *Charlotte's Web*. HarperCollins.

* _____. *Stuart Little*. HarperCollins.

* Williams, Margery. *The Velveteen Rabbit*. HarperCollins.

Some Other Books by Kate DiCamillo

* *Because of Winn-Dixie*. Candlewick Press.

* *Tale of Despereaux*. Candlewick Press.

* *The Tiger Raising*. Candlewick Press.

* NOVEL-TIES Study Guides are available for these titles.

ANSWER KEY

Chapters 1 – 4
Vocabulary: 1. d 2. e 3. f 4. g 5. h 6. a 7. b 8. c; 1. unsavory 2. duration 3. grotesque 4. diligence 5. implications 6. china 7. jaunty 8. specimen
Questions: 1. It was clear that Abilene considered Edward to be "real" by the way she spoke to him as if he were a person, dressed him in new outfits, and brought him to the dinner table, where she expected her family to include him in the conversation. 2. Edward didn't like Abilene's parents, nor most other adults, because they talked down to him and they didn't talk about the only subject he was interested in—himself. 3. Edward was always awake because his eyes were painted open. 4. When Rosie attacked, Edward did not feel pain, but was outraged for being treated with great indignity. 5. Edward was upset because the maid treated him like any ordinary object that needed dusting and cleaning. He was insulted that she vacuumed his ears and stashed him on the shelf in an unflattering pose. 6. Abilene was unhappy about the ending of Pellegrina's story because the Princess was shot and the story did not end happily ever after. 7. Pellegrina understood that Edward was selfish and unloving; Abilene did not really understand her rabbit because, loving him so much, she assumed that he was loving, too.

Chapters 5 – 9
Vocabulary: 1. frantic–desperate; wildly excited 2. singular–quite unusual 3. mortified–deeply embarrassed 4. blithely–cheerfully; gaily 5. descent–downward movement 6. pummeled–beat as if with a fist 7. discerning–thoughtful; perceptive
Questions: 1. Edward was glad that Pellegrina was not going on the trip because he knew she was critical of him. 2. Edward ended up at the bottom of the ocean when some mischievous boys on the *Queen Mary* began tossing him around: in the shuffle, the rabbit went overboard. 3. Edward's first true emotion was the fear that he felt lying on the ocean floor after being tossed overboard by the boys aboard the ship. 4. Edward was rescued by a fisherman who caught him in his net. The fisherman handled Edward carefully so that his wife would be able to repair it. 5. Edward was confused when Nellie referred to him as "she." 6. Nellie had experienced the great sadness of losing her young son to pneumonia. 7. Edward felt that life with Nellie and Lawrence was good because they treated him kindly; he was able to easily adjust to the new life, even to becoming "Susanna," because he mostly thought of his own comforts and so did not greatly miss Abilene or his old way of life. 8. Edward blamed Pellegrina for his troubles, feeling that she was somehow punishing him by bringing misfortune on him. 9. Lawrence showed his fondness for "Susanna" by speaking to the rabbit and taking the rabbit out to see the constellations in the night sky.

Chapters 10 – 15
Vocabulary: 1. a 2. c 3. f 4. b 5. e 6. d; 1. exhilarated 2. resonated 3. abiding 4. savor 5. garb 6. rancid
Questions: 1. Edward formed an immediate hatred for Lolly because her appearance seemed garish to him and her actions were violent, particularly when she threw him into the garbage. 2. Lolly took Edward to the dump because she thought that her parents' loving treatment of Edward made them look odd and foolish in the eyes of the neighbors. 3. Edward realized that he had changed because he now understood that in the past, he had failed to return Abilene's love for him. 4. A dog dug into the garbage heap where Edward was buried, shook off the garbage on him, and rescued him from Ernest, who claimed to be king of the Garbages. 5. Edward ended up on the road with a hobo because the dog that rescued him from the dump brought him to Bull, his master: Bull took a liking to the doll and decided to take him along as he traveled. 6. Like all hoboes, Bull's journey did not have a destination. He was constantly moving to stay away from the authorities. 7. Bull felt the need to change Edward's clothes because the dress he was wearing was in tatters and also seemed too fancy for their travels. 8. Listening to other people's stories opened Edward's heart because he was beginning to identify with feelings of love and loss. 9. A railroad worker, checking the freight cars, became infuriated when he saw Bull, the dog Lucy, and the doll inside. In a rage he tossed Edward out of the moving train; thus, separating Edward from Bull. 10. What made Edward feel that he had "done with caring" was his despair at being made into a lonely scarecrow who meant nothing to anyone.

Chapters 16 – 19
Vocabulary: 1. d 2. e 3. f 4. a 5. h 6. c 7. b 8. g; 1. ignored 2. prevailed 3. provoked 4. loathed 5. intrusive 6. tentative 7. murmured 8. refused
Questions: 1. Bryce rescued Edward because he knew his little sister, who was sick, would appreciate having a toy to replace the doll her father had smashed to pieces. 2. Sarah Ruth treated Edward like

a baby; Edward responded well to her attentions because, after his loneliness and humiliation as a scarecrow, he needed to be comforted and babied. 3. The new feeling Edward experienced with Sarah Ruth was the desire to offer his comfort and protection; he felt this way because Sarah was sick and helpless. 4. Details in the story that showed the family's poverty were the tiny, bare shack they lived in; the lack of a doctor for Sarah Ruth; the lack of food; and the absence of toys. 5. Bryce attached strings to Edward so that he could make him dance like a marionette in order to entertain Sarah Ruth. 6. Bryce, the older brother, played the role of father to Sarah Ruth, feeding her, watching over her, and making her as comfortable as possible. 7. Bryce set off for Memphis because he could not get along with his father; he had stayed at home long enough to care for his beloved little sister. Once she died, there was no reason for him to stay at home.

Chapters 20 – 23

Vocabulary: Across—4. encourage 6. restore 7. assistance 8. constellation 9. oblivion 10. shuffle; Down—1. elegant 2. magnificent 3. sorrow 4. exceedingly 5. continually

Questions: 1. Edward felt hollow again because he had lost his connection to Sarah Ruth, the girl he'd grown to love. 2. Bryce made Edward dance in public to earn money for food as they traveled to Memphis. 3. Edward identified the old woman with the cane as Pellegrina because she gave him the same piercing look that Pellegrina had given him years before. 4. Neal swung Edward against the counter because he became enraged when Bryce could not pay his bill. This caused Edward's head to crack into many pieces. 5. Edward's world "went black," meant that Edward lost consciousness. 6. In Chapter Twenty-two, the events were all part of Edward's jumbled dream; Edward was dreaming of all the people he'd loved and lost, and his enduring wish to be able to fly. 7. Bryce sacrificed his own need for Edward as his companion and source of income so that the doll could receive the expensive repair that he could not afford. 8. Lucius Clarke mended Edward because he hoped to make a profit from his expert restoration once he found a buyer.

Chapters 24 – Coda

Vocabulary: 1. shattered–the other words are alike because they are all synonyms for *fixed* 2. glum–the other words are alike because they all mean arrogant 3. precious–the other words are alike because they all mean evident 4. mild–the other words are alike because they all refer to a state of strong feeling about something or someone 5. occupied–the other words are alike because they all mean "without contents" 6. pleasant–the other words are alike because they all describe something that is distasteful 7. jokingly–the other words are alike because they all refer to a thoughtful, serious state 8. robust–the other words are alike because they all mean easily broken or shattered

Questions: 1. Lucius didn't want Bryce to keep returning to his shop because he thought the boy would only upset himself by looking at the rabbit he had once possessed but now had given up. 2. Edward said he didn't want anyone to buy him because he was afraid to hope for love again. 3. The hundred-year-old doll tried to explain to Edward that love was the reason for living; Pellegrina had tried to explain this to Edward long before. 4. Edward dared to hope again for love when the old doll was purchased by a little girl who was looking for a friend, rather than for a fancy doll; he was also encouraged by the old doll's words, "Someone will come for you." 5. Abilene recognized Edward when her daughter expressed an intense desire for the china rabbit; when Abilene looked more closely, she recognized her long-lost Edward. 6. Abilene wore Edward's old pocket watch the way people usually wear a locket; she wore it because she had never forgotten Edward. 7. The story ended "happily ever after" as Edward found a home with the adult Abilene, who had loved him all these years, and her daughter Maggie with whom it was love at first sight.